BLACKPOOL TO FLEETWOOD BY TRAM
A 40 YEAR JOURNEY

MIKE RHODES

AMBERLEY

Acknowledgements

Thanks to Ian McLoughlin for checking the factual content of the manuscript.

Bibliography

Palmer, Steve and Brian Turner, *Trams and Buses around Blackpool* (Blackpool, Palmer & Turner, 1982).
Palmer, Steve, *Century of Trams* (Blackpool Borough Council, 1985).
Palmer, Steve, *Blackpool & Fleetwood by Tram* (Sheffield, Platform 5 Publishing Ltd, 1988).
Fylde Tramway Society Bulletins (various).

First published 2022

Amberley Publishing
The Hill, Stroud
Gloucestershire, GL5 4EP

www.amberley-books.com

Copyright © Mike Rhodes, 2022

The right of Mike Rhodes to be identified as the Author of this work has been asserted in accordance with the Copyrights, Designs and Patents Act 1988.

ISBN 978 1 3981 0842 4 (print)
ISBN 978 1 3981 0843 1 (ebook)

British Library Cataloguing in Publication Data.
A catalogue record for this book is available from the British Library.

Origination by Amberley Publishing.
Printed in the UK.

Introduction

Blackpool began to flourish as a destination for day trippers and holidaymakers in the second half of the nineteenth century. The first railway across the Fylde was opened from Preston to Fleetwood in July 1840. Blackpool was initially served by a branch from this line which diverged at Poulton-le-Fylde and opened in April 1846. By the end of the century thousands of people flocked to the resort during the summer months. To cater for the explosion in rail traffic a second, more direct, line was opened from Kirkham to Blackpool in 1903. Blackpool then had three main railway stations situated at North, Central and South.

The first section of tramway was laid along the south Promenade between Cocker Street and Station Road. It was constructed mainly as a single line (with passing places) using standard-gauge track and was operated by electric trams that picked up current from a conduit laid between the rails. Known as the Blackpool Electric Tramway Company, it opened for business on 29 September 1885. The line was purchased by Blackpool Corporation seven years later and extensions were laid along Lytham Road, Squires Gate Lane and Station Road. The initial tram depot was situated in Blundell Street; the access was from Princess Street and it was built to house the original fleet of eight four-wheel cars and two trailers.

Meanwhile on 1 July 1898 the Blackpool and Fleetwood Tramroad Company (B&FTC) commenced operation of an electric tramway from Bold Street in Fleetwood to Dickson Road in Blackpool (North station). Depots were established at Bold Street (with a capacity for only four cars), Copse Road and Bispham. Unlike the Blackpool system the electrical current was taken from an overhead wire. The Blackpool conduit system was fraught with problems due to its exposure to the sea elements and consequently it was resolved to convert the whole of the network to overhead current collection, in 1899.

Further extensions to the system were made between 1900 and 1902 when lines were opened along the north Promenade to Gynn Square, from Talbot Square to Lytham Road via Marton (including a new depot) and to Layton. The Blackpool Tramway was also connected to the Blackpool St Annes & Lytham Tramway Company at Squires Gate Lane, with the latter having commenced operation of their own electric trams in 1903 following a period of operation with gas-powered trams. Tram depots were located in Henry Street in Lytham (closed in 1903) and Squires Gate Lane, which remained open to the end of the tramway operation in April 1937 and was later used as a bus garage. It was finally vacated sixty-two years later.

Following the expiry of the B&FTC's lease at the end of 1919, the system was acquired by Blackpool Corporation on 1 January 1920, thus enabling the latter to run trams from South Pier to Fleetwood for the first time. Bold Street depot was not taken on by the Corporation and passed into private ownership, but the building was not demolished until 1973. The system was further extended in 1924–26 when lines were laid from Bold Street via Queen's Terrace and Pharos Street to North Albert Street in Fleetwood and between South Pier and Starr Gate. The tramway had now reached its most expansive form with in excess of 17 route miles.

Following overhead electrification and expansion of the system, which included the enlargement of Blundell Street depot to accommodate a maximum of forty-five cars, a fleet of twenty

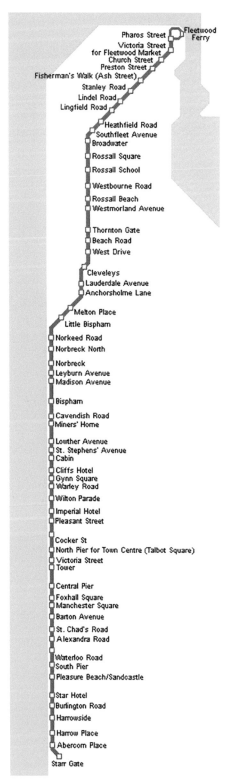

Pharos Street
Fleetwood Ferry
Victoria Street for Fleetwood Market
Church Street
Preston Street
Fisherman's Walk (Ash Street)
Stanley Road
Lindel Road
Lingfield Road
Heathfield Road
Southfleet Avenue
Broadwater
Rossall Square
Rossall School
Westbourne Road
Rossall Beach
Westmorland Avenue
Thornton Gate
Beach Road
West Drive
Cleveleys
Lauderdale Avenue
Anchorsholme Lane
Melton Place
Little Bispham
Norkeed Road
Norbreck North
Norbreck
Leyburn Avenue
Madison Avenue
Bispham
Cavendish Road
Miners' Home
Lowther Avenue
St. Stephens' Avenue
Cabin
Cliffs Hotel
Gynn Square
Warley Road
Wilton Parade
Imperial Hotel
Pleasant Street
Cocker St
North Pier for Town Centre (Talbot Square)
Victoria Street
Tower
Central Pier
Foxhall Square
Manchester Square
Barton Avenue
St. Chad's Road
Alexandra Road
Waterloo Road
South Pier
Pleasure Beach/Sandcastle
Star Hotel
Burlington Road
Harrowside
Harrow Place
Abercom Place
Starr Gate

The Blackpool Tramway before the pattern of stops was rationalised for the LRT in 2012.

high-capacity Dreadnought trams, built by G. F. Milnes, was purchased to operate the enhanced services. These were later supplemented by fifteen double-deck cars known as Marton Box Cars and later, in 1911–14, the Corporation bought twenty-four Toastrack trams to operate on tours and promenade extras. These then formed the nucleus of the fleet until the start of the 1920s.

Upon acquisition of the B&FTC an additional forty-one cars of Milnes & United Electric Car Company manufacture were taken into stock. A few years later Blackpool embarked on a programme of constructing their own double-deck trams, which became known as Standards. Forty-two of the type (which included seven built by Hurst Nelson of Motherwell) entered service between 1923 and 1929. Six more Toastracks were also constructed at Rigby Road in 1927 and a batch of ten stylish single-deck cars, officially known as Pullman's but generally referred to as Pantograph cars, was obtained from Dick, Kerr in Preston the following year. By the early 1930s the Dreadnoughts and acquired B&FTC trams were life expired and passenger numbers were increasing significantly. Modernisation and further fleet expansion was clearly needed.

In November 1932 the council appointed Walter Luff as their new general manager. Luff was responsible for both the trams and the buses and he had the same vision for both modes of transport – to enhance both fleets with striking new streamlined vehicles. It was at this time that the livery was changed from red and white to green and cream. The English Electric Company Works (EE) in Preston was charged with constructing eighty-four new trams of three basic types – forty-five single-deck saloons known as Railcoaches; twelve open-top saloons which acquired the name of Open-boats; and twenty-seven double-deck cars which later became known as 'Balloons'. The latter were a mixture of closed and open-top trams. All the new trams entered service between 1933 and 1935 and were housed in a new depot which was constructed at Rigby Road. Opened in 1935 it contained seventeen roads and had a capacity for 102 of the new larger trams.

Such was the popularity of Blackpool as a holiday destination that more new trams were purchased before the outbreak of the Second World War. Twenty more Railcoaches, built by Brush Electrical Engineering of Loughborough, but almost identical to the EE design, were followed by a further twelve saloons from English Electric, which were later fitted with VAMBAC control equipment, giving rise to the name Marton Vambacs (following their use on the Marton route). For the next twenty years the Streamliners and Standards formed the backbone of the tram fleet until the Coronation cars were purchased from Charles Roberts of Horbury in 1952/3. Twenty-five in number, these replaced a number of Standards but were destined to have a relatively short life with the Transport Department.

The 1950s and the early years of the 1960s brought about a second renaissance for the resort as the UK population was finally released from the last vestiges of wartime restrictions. The phrase 'Always a tram in sight' was coined and was indeed true as processions of packed trams could be seen plying their trade between the Pleasure Beach and Little Bispham. The start of the swinging sixties also heralded more innovations as the Corporation fashioned a number of individual illuminated trams and rebuilt ten of the Railcoaches as motor sets, which were permanently coupled to newly built trailers and designated as Progress Twin-Cars.

Between the years 1955 and 1970 the size of the tram fleet was slimmed down from 166 to 106 with the closure of the remaining street sections of tramway and the resultant withdrawal of the Series One Railcoaches, the Marton Vambacs and the last remaining Standards. The depots at Bispham, Copse Road and Marton were also closed during this period. In 1968 the tram fleet was renumbered into the 6xx/7xx series. With declining passenger numbers throughout the 1970s it was decided to convert the remaining English Electric-built Railcoaches into 'OPO (one-person operated)' trams; a process which required significant alterations to the cabs. Thirteen conversions were done between 1972 and 1976 and these were generally the only trams to be seen out on the Starr Gate to Fleetwood service during the winter months.

Attention then turned to rebuilding some of the Balloon cars for 'OPO' but in the event only two, Nos 714/25, were done, becoming Nos 762/1 respectively. By 1983 the size of the tram fleet had been reduced to eighty-three. A combination of the deteriorating condition of the track and the prolonged overhang of the converted 'OPO' Railcoaches was taking its toll on the type and a replacement tram was sought in the mid-1980s. This emerged as the Centenary tram, of which eight (one of which was modified from a GEC test tram) were built between 1984 and 1987. They had East Lancashire Coachbuilder's bodies mounted on Blackpool trucks and powered by English Electric motors. The last of the 'OPO' cars ran in 1993. Blundell Street depot, which for many years had latterly been used as a storage shed, was closed and demolished in 1982.

A limited company, Blackpool Transport Services, was formed in 1986 with responsibility for the buses and trams and the undertaking has remained council owned ever since. Throughout the 1990s and 2000s the company had to soldier on with very little investment in the tramway. The trams, many of which dated from the 1930s, were somehow kept running but there were casualties along the way. Over a six year period from 1998 to 2004 four Balloons were extensively modified with redesigned flat fronts. However in 2004 twenty-five trams, which were deemed to be surplus to requirements, were put into cold storage. Just how bad the situation had become was exemplified by the service offered between January and April 2007, with a turnout of just four trams that operated a truncated service between Thornton Gate and Fleetwood. The rest of the line was closed for essential maintenance. That year the winter service was withdrawn in its entirety, with no trams running for the first time in the tramway's then 122 year existence.

The gloom started to lift in February 2008 when Blackpool Council was awarded £85.3 million to upgrade the whole of the tramway to Light Rail Transit standard. This sum included £25 million, which was provided equally by both Lancashire County and Blackpool Borough councils. Over the next three years large sections of the line were re-laid and a new depot was built at Starr Gate. It was designed to accommodate twenty of Bombardier's Flexity 2 articulated trams, of which Blackpool ordered sixteen (two additional trams were acquired in December 2017) and was the initial recipient of the model. The new depot incorporated many sustainable features such as surface water drainage attenuation and natural lighting and it was equipped with a large workshop area to maintain the trams. As part of the upgrade work thirty-eight new tram stops, with raised platforms, were constructed, replacing the sixty-one previous stopping places which over certain sections had been much closer together.

The new LRT system commenced operation on 4 April 2012. An extension to the tramway, linking Talbot Square with North railway station had been partly constructed at the time of writing. While the new trams form the core service, around fifty of the old trams, of which around twenty are operational and fairly representative of most of the types operated over the years, are housed at the Rigby Road depot. A new heritage trust was formed in July 2014 with overall responsibility for the heritage trams, buildings and artefacts. Heritage trams are now operated on a frequent basis using volunteer crews. The heritage service is generally confined to the section of line between the Pleasure Beach and Little Bispham although Fleetwood is also reached when an enhanced service is provided on 'Gold' weekends. These trams only call at a small number of designated stops which don't have raised access.

In its 136 year history the Blackpool Tramway has had many ups and downs. The 11-mile-long, mainly coastal, line which exists today is a testament to all who have worked so hard over the years to keep it running. This pictorial account traces the route of the line from south to north and features the majority of the trams that have operated over the line, including many visiting trams, during the past forty years. Virtually all of the pictures featured were taken by the author, who retains copyright. Enjoy!

Mike Rhodes

The extension to the line from South Pier to Starr Gate was only constructed in 1926 and originally terminated in a double stub-end arrangement, although a connecting line was also provided along the middle of the adjacent road to Squires Gate Lane. The layout was altered in 1938 with trams turning by way of a single line loop. Built by English Electric (EE), Balloon car No. 717 (originally No. 254) was new in December 1934. It is seen at the Starr Gate tram stop on 11 July 1978 with One Person Operated 'OPO' car No. 6 and similar Balloon No. 720.

Between 1972 and 1976 thirteen of the English Electric Railcoaches were rebuilt for 'OPO'. The modification included the provision of an additional entrance doorway at either end. No. 5 was modified from No. 221, which was latterly used as a permanent way vehicle, and entered service in its new guise in November 1972. By the time of this view, taken on 5 June 1982 leaving Starr Gate, No. 5 had been fitted with a single-arm pantograph. These were the only trams to carry the red and cream livery. It lasted in service until February 1993 and is now part of the Crich Tramway Museum collection.

In conjunction with the construction of a new tram depot at Starr Gate the boarding arrangements for the new Light Rail Vehicles (LRVs) was substantially altered. The arrangement of two raised platforms followed the pattern which was adopted for the whole of the new tramway. The first of the new LRVs, No. 001, is seen at Starr Gate on 10 August 2012. These impressive articulated trams were built at Bombardier's factory in Bautzen in Germany and transported across Europe by road to Rotterdam and then by ferry to Hull and finally across the Pennines by way of the M62 and M61.

Seen waiting to leave Starr Gate for Fleetwood Ferry at 18.30 on 1 December 2017 is LRV Flexity 2 No. 008. The new layout was again formed of a turning loop with a single line that passed through the confines of the depot yard with trams now turning by way of an anti-clockwise manoeuvre.

Above and below: The new tram depot was designed and constructed by VolkerFitzpatrick and was located on land adjacent to the sea wall, which had latterly housed a go-kart track and a car park. Work began on site in late 2009 and the building was ready for use by September 2011. Ten roads were provided, each with a capacity to hold two trams. The three roads on the west side are equipped for maintenance of the trams with an arrangement of pits and gantries to access all the components of the trams. The remaining seven roads are located on the opposite side of the offices and facilities rooms. The illuminated view from the outside was taken on 1 December 2017 while the internal view, which features LRVs Nos 008 and 001, was recorded on 13 September 2017. No. 008 on the left has been placed on jacks and all three sets of bogies have been removed for a detailed inspection to be carried out of all the individual components.

The holiday season was well underway when this picture of 'OPO' car No. 6 (617/270) was taken on 5 June 1982. The tram is seen on the final stretch of straight track before it reaches Starr Gate. When first (re)built Nos 1–9 were painted plum and custard which was short lived and later replaced by red and cream. No. 6 was withdrawn following the arrival of the Centenary trams in the mid-1980s and was scrapped soon afterwards.

No. 700 (originally Nos 237/226) was the first of the new streamlined 'Balloon' cars to be received, in February 1934. It was originally an open-top tram but, along with the rest of the batch, the top deck was enclosed in 1942. It was splendidly restored to this green and cream wartime livery in the 1990s, regaining its original twin destination screens. It is seen approaching the Harrow Place tram stop on 25 June 2007.

Three Balloon cars, Nos 700/11/9, all of which had previously been modified with widened doors, were painted in the LRT colours of white and purple. No. 711 (248) is seen at Harrow Place on 31 August 2015. The intention was that these trams would be available to supplement the LRV service, but they have rarely been used in such a capacity.

Meanwhile looking in the opposite direction on 5 June 2018, Brush Railcoach No. 623 (286), which was new in July 1937, was restored to wartime green and cream colours in 2007 following a brief period in store. It was withdrawn in 2009 and later passed to the Heaton Park Tramway in Manchester. No. 623 is passing LRV Flexity 2 No. 012 during a period of loan to the BHT; it returned to Heaton Park in July 2018. Featured in the background is the 'Big One' rollercoaster, standing at 213 feet tall.

Blackpool's Pleasure Beach amusement theme park moved to its present site in 1923. The first section of tramway, opened in 1885, terminated close to this location and two additional lengths of straight track were laid to cater for the large number of extra trams which served the attraction. LRV Flexity 2 No. 002 is seen on 31 August 2015.

The layout at the Pleasure Beach terminus was not altered until the 1930s when a double line turning loop was constructed to provide additional capacity; a single straight loop was also retained alongside the running lines. English Electric Balloon car No. 703 (240) has terminated at the Pleasure Beach on 13 October 1990. New in September 1934, No. 703 continued in service until 2009 when it was painted red and cream and preserved in the guise of a Sunderland Corporation tram. Following a period of operation at the Beamish Living Museum it was returned to Blackpool in March 2017 and placed into store.

Another scene at the Pleasure Beach was recorded on 13 October 1990. 'OPO' car No. 8 (612/265) is on the outer loop line while Progress Twin-Car No. 682+672 and Balloon No. 719 (256) occupy the inner loop. The Twin-Car entered service in August 1960 formed of rebuilt Railcoach No. 272 and newly constructed Trailer T2 (682).

Balloon car No. 716 (253) is seen at the Pleasure Beach on 6 August 1983. No. 716 entered service in March 1935 and continued in use until 2003 when it was placed in store requiring a new underframe. It was later sold and departed Blackpool in 2010 for a new home in Perth in Scotland and has since been scrapped.

Above and below: These two scenes were recorded on 25 September 2016 during the autumn heritage weekend extravaganza. Boat car No. 600 (225) is in a spot of bother having partially derailed on the points and has attracted a crowd while attempts are made to re-rail the errant tram. No. 600 enjoyed a spell of use at the Heaton Park Tramway from 1985–97. It was last overhauled in 2009 and has been a regular performer since September 2010. Meanwhile Balloon No. 718 (255) was one of four of the type rebuilt with flat ends (as shown below) and classified as Millennium cars. It was later modified with widened entrances for use on the LRT system. Having previously carried only all-over adverts since its modification it was painted white and placed at the disposal of the heritage fleet. Eventually it was painted green and cream in 2017.

Twenty more Railcoaches were supplied by Brush Engineering of Loughborough in 1937. Around a dozen of these survived in service until the twenty-first century. No. 627 (290) was withdrawn from general service in November 2004 but was brought out of retirement to perform a last day tour in November 2009. Now owned by the Fleetwood Heritage Leisure Trust (FHLT) it was in store at Rigby Road in 2020. It is seen opposite the theme park, where at one time there used to be four tracks, on 14 September 1985.

No. 40 was built by the United Electric Car Co. of Preston and delivered to the B&FTC in 1914. Renumbered to 114, following the takeover by the company by Blackpool Corporation in January 1920, it was withdrawn from service in October 1936 and subsequently used as a service car. It was first partly restored for the 75th anniversary celebrations in 1960. Now resident at the Crich Tramway Museum it had a long spell on the Blackpool tramway which extended from 1996 to 2019.

This line-up on the Pleasure Beach loop on 26 October 2017 features illuminated trams Nos 737 (Trawler), 736 (Frigate) and 734/3 (Western Train). No. 737 is the most recent addition to the feature cars, entering service in 2001, and was built using parts from withdrawn Railcoach No. 633 (296). The Frigate dates from 1965 and was fashioned out of Pantograph car No. 170 while the Western Train entered service in 1962 with Railcoach No. 209 (later replaced by No. 277/677) and Pantograph car No. 174 providing the basis for the two sections.

Balloon car No. 715 (252) was one of the last unmodified trams of its type to remain in service. Repainted into the 1970s green and cream livery it is seen at the Pleasure Beach on the last night of conventional tramway operation, 6 November 2011, waiting to depart on a Fylde Tramway Society Tour. It rejoined the BTS fleet in 2013 and was repainted into the 1990s livery before re-entering service with the heritage trust in May 2015.

There were originally twelve English Electric-built Open Boat cars which entered service in the summer of 1934. Four of the type were scrapped at Blundell Street in 1968, while by 2013 a further four had crossed the Atlantic to the USA. No. 607 (236) is seen on the Pleasure Beach loop on 13 October 1990; it was moved to the Crich Tramway Museum in April 2012. In the background is the Sandcastle Waterpark, which opened in 1986 and was built on the site of a former municipal open-air swimming pool.

While the inner loop line at the Pleasure Beach was traversed anti-clockwise, trams on the outer loop line proceeded clockwise. Balloon cars Nos 712 (249) and 702 (239) are displaying different livery applications in this 11 September 2004 view and are waiting in turn for the dispatcher's signal to move off. No. 712 also moved to the museum in Crich, in March 2010, having been one of the last of its type in regular service.

Freshly out-shopped Balloon No. 720 (257) is seen arriving at the Pleasure Beach on 23 April 1984. This livery style was a deviation from what had been the norm throughout the 1970s and early 1980s and lasted until a further change was made at the beginning of the next decade. It was refurbished in 2010 with various modifications but was among the stored items of rolling stock in 2020.

The Twin-Cars were ideal for moving large crowds to and from the Pleasure Beach. No. 674+684 (274+T4) is seen taking on a healthy load on 14 September 1985 but is purporting to be only going as far as Manchester Square. These double-trams also required two conductors, as did the Balloons. This set was last reported to be with the North Eastern Electric Traction Trust (NEETT) near Sunderland, having departed Blackpool in July 2012.

For a spell LRV Flexity 2 No. 016 carried this advert for Fleetwood Freeport before it received a different advert in 2018 (see page 46). This broadside view was recorded outside the Sandcastle Waterpark on 27 September 2015. These impressive looking trams are 32.2 metres long and have a total capacity to convey 222 passengers (seventy-four seated).

Edinburgh Corporation Tramways No. 35 was built at the ECT works at Shrubhill in Leith Walk and entered service in 1948. It was fitted with Peckham P22 trucks. Latterly working from Tollcross depot it was withdrawn from service in October 1956. No. 35 had an extended period of loan to the Blackpool Tramway in the mid-1980s and was included in the line-up for the centenary parade in September 1985. It is seen between South and Central piers on 23 April 1984 and is about to pass Balloon car No. 702 (239).

The Western Train, Nos 733/4, has been delighting visitors and enthusiasts alike for nigh on sixty years. It is seen on the South Shore, opposite Radcliffe Street, on 26 October 2017, with the Frigate and Trawler in close pursuit. On reaching the Tower the trio formed a backdrop for a brief performance by a colourful dance troop before completing a tour of the lights.

A little further along the Promenade, opposite Alexandra Road, Brush Railcoach No. 634 (297) is seen passing modified EE Railcoach No. 679 (279) on 13 October 1990. By this time, other than the boat cars, very few of the trams retained their trolley poles. In 2020 No. 634 was in store at Rigby Road while No. 679 was under restoration at the Brinwell Road workshops in nearby Marton. Both had been withdrawn at the end of the 2004 season.

Above and below: Although taken from opposite sides of the tracks these two pictures feature trams at the same location – St Chad's Road tram stop. In the picture above, Balloon cars Nos 708 (245) and 712 (249) are seen heading for the Pleasure Beach on 27 June 1981 while below we see LRV Flexity No. 002 on 27 September 2015 with a service for Fleetwood. Not much has changed as there is now only a shelter on the northbound platform as the southbound platform is not wide enough to accommodate one. No. 708 last ran in service in 2004 and first departed Rigby Road depot in November 2011. It is now owned by the Heaton Park Tramway, but returned to Rigby Road in September 2016 for storage. The white and purple colours of the LRVs are the same as the colours displayed on Blackpool Council's vehicle fleet.

Four of the Twin-Car sets remained at Rigby Road depot in 2020, two of which have seen service with the heritage fleet. Set No. 672+682 was returned to service in September 2012 in its original livery and displaying its original numbers of 272+T2. Although out of service in 2020 it had also been used in recent years as a driver training tram. It is seen at St Chad's Road on 31 August 2015.

The next stop heading north was at Barton Avenue, which was not included in the tramway upgrade. Open trams Nos 605 (233) and 706 (243) portray the very essence of a seaside resort on a hot summer's day – recorded on 2 June 1985. No. 706 was rebuilt to its original open-top format following an accident in July 1980. Out of service since 2015, *Princess Alice*, as it was named four days later, was awaiting a body overhaul in 2020.

The majority of the Standard trams were built in the department's own workshops at Rigby Road between 1923 and 1929. However No. 147 was built by Hurst Nelson of Motherwell in 1924 and was one of the last to remain in service being withdrawn in 1966. It was then sold for preservation in the USA but returned to the UK in October 2000 and eventually re-entered service in 2002. Now part of the heritage fleet it was photographed on the South Shore on 27 September 2015 bound for the Pleasure Beach.

The twenty Brush-built Railcoaches, numbered 284–303, entered service in the summer of 1937. Numbers 301 and 303 were scrapped in 1968 and 1963 respectively while the remainder became Nos 621–638. The majority were modified with single destination boxes in the 1970s. Seen near Manchester Square on 27 June 1981, No. 630 (293) was withdrawn in October 2011 and then passed to the Tramway Museum at Crich. It returned to Blackpool for a loan spell between September 2017 and April 2019.

Balloon car No. 706 (243), before its accident, is seen in Lytham Road leaving the depot for service on 3 July 1976. It was the last but one of the batch to receive a single indicator box, in December 1972. Having originally been an open-top tram it was rebuilt as such again in 1985 and was named *Princess Alice* by the Princess on 6 June 1985.

Blackpool Tramways celebrated its centenary in 1985 and a grand parade of trams was assembled on the Promenade on 29 September. One of the stars of the show was Blackpool Conduit car No. 4. It was built by the Lancaster Railway Carriage & Wagon Co. and entered service on the opening day of the tramway in September 1885. It was withdrawn in 1905 but continued as a Works car for another thirty years. After a period of storage it was restored in 1960. After being displayed at the Museum of Transport in Clapham it moved to Crich in April 1979. It is seen in Lytham Road, now powered by a single electric motor and chain driven, on the day of the centenary parade.

The Centenary class of purpose-built 'OPO' cars was first introduced in 1985 although, what became No. 648, and was originally a test tram with GEC motors and numbered 651, preceded them. Three of the type were part of the heritage fleet in 2020, No. 642 having been returned to service in August 2018. It is in Hopton Road, leaving the depot, on 22 September 2018. It is advertising the various types of heritage tickets available.

In this view, taken on 27 June 1981, the trams present a uniform appearance, before all-over advert schemes and livery variations became all the rage. Seven of the Balloon cars can be seen with Nos 711 (248) and 702 (239) at the front of the line. Brush Railcoach No. 627 is alongside with 'OPO' Jubilee car No. 761 (ex-725) to the right of one of the single-deck 'OPO' cars. When opened in 1935, Rigby Road depot had seventeen parking roads, each with a capacity to hold six of the then new streamlined cars.

Above and below: The tram workshops at Rigby Road were opened in 1920 and pre-date the operation of motorbuses. In 2020 the surviving building contained a body repair shop, a paint shop, a machine shop and a store room that contained spare parts for the buses. Both the body and repair shops were also used by the modern day buses. Standard car No. 147 was present in the paint shop on 18 September 2017 while Birkenhead Tramways No. 20 was receiving attention in the machine shop on 10 October 2017. No. 20 was built at the G. F. Miles' factory in Birkenhead and operated on the town's tramway between 1901 and 1937, when the system closed. In one corner of this extensive shop is a fully equipped Blacksmiths' forge which was installed when the building was first built. Should the Trust achieve charitable status then various aspects of the old tramway facilities at Rigby Road could be opened up to the general public to view. There was also an electrical compound in the main depot which occupied tracks 16 and 17.

On 22 July 1980 Balloon cars Nos 705 (242) and 706 (243) collided head-on at the Pleasure Beach. Both were initially stored and while No. 705 was ultimately scrapped, in October 1982, No. 706 languished at the depot a good while longer before the decision was taken to rebuild it back to its original form as an open-top tram. It is seen dumped in the bus yard on 2 July 1983 with withdrawn Brush Railcoach No. 638 (302). Withdrawn in May 1980, No. 638 was eventually scrapped in March 1984.

The illuminated trams have been a feature of tramway operations for many decades. The present crop of trams mainly date back to the early 1960s. On 7 October 1978 No. 732 *The Rocket* was photographed at the entrance to the depot. It was built on the underframe of Pantograph car No. 168 and entered service in 1961. It has not operated since 1999.

Above and below: Two views of trams inside the depot which were recorded nearly thirty years apart. In the picture above, which was taken on 4 July 1982, one of the recently built Jubilee trams takes centre stage. No. 762 had only entered service a few weeks earlier and had been constructed from Balloon car No. 714. The two Jubilee trams differed in a number of respects. Whereas No. 761 had a front entrance/exit, No. 762 had exit doors in the centre. Also the seating capacity of the latter was eight fewer, at ninety. Behind No. 761 can be seen the Dreadnought and the Western Train while the Post Office Railcoach, No. 633, is alongside. The Metro Coastlines concept of route branding was introduced in April 2001 and livery applications also spread to the trams. On 27 September 2010 Balloon car No. 715 was displaying a version of this while No. 706, *Princess Alice*, sits behind with the Frigate on the left. Ironically the Metro concept was dropped in that year.

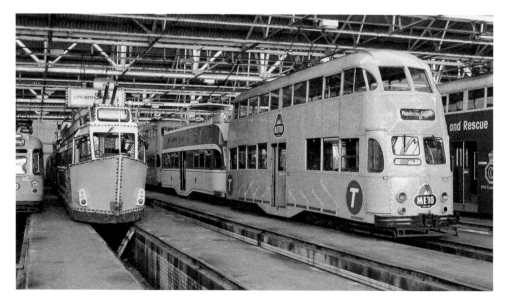

This view, taken on 5 June 1982, is an abject study in front ends. Although modified destination apertures have been fitted, Balloon car No. 717 (254) and Brush Railcoach No. 637 (300) aptly portray Luff's streamline effect. These contrast with the squarer appearance of rebuilt Railcoach No. 675 (the powered half of Twin-Car No. 675+685). Finally the vastly different profile of preserved Dreadnought tram No. 59, which dates from 1902, contrasts markedly with the other three.

On 30 April 2018 the view inside the depot was somewhat different. Now in use as an operational base for the heritage cars the trams on show reflected the buildings altered function. Brush Railcoaches Nos 621/30 represented different eras of the tramway operation while Blackpool & Fleetwood Box No. 40 dates back to 1914. Also on view is multi-purpose Works car No. 754. Both Nos 40 and 630 were operating on loan from Crich Tramway Museum at the time.

On 14 July 1991, Balloon car No. 710 (247) was photographed passing through the automated washer. The washer was actually located in Hopton Road and the two segments were mounted on wheels to enable them to be moved. This arrangement was done away with following the cessation of the old tramway operation and the heritage trams are now generally hand washed or occasionally pass through the washer at the Starr Gate LRV depot.

Rigby Road depot after dark and in the wet, as seen on 19 October 2017. The trams on view, under cover, are unrestored Railcoaches Nos 625/32, Balloon cars Nos 715/7, restored modified EE Railcoach No. 680 and Brush Railcoach No. 621. Feature car No. 737, *The Trawler*, is ready to depart for a tour of the Illuminations.

This combination of Works vehicles depicts Brush Railcoach No. 624 (287), which was withdrawn from normal service in 1971, and rail carrier No. 751, which was basically the modified underframe of former Railcoach No. 628 (291) and which last saw service as a tram in 1969. The pair, seen in Blundell Street on 11 July 1978, were normally engaged on the transportation of rails from Thornton Gate PW depot.

Balloon cars Nos 703/6 (240/3) are seen on display in Blundell Street on 22 September 2018. The latter is painted in a non-authentic version of the Sunderland Corporation Tramways livery, having previously been in use at the Beamish Living Museum. In 2020 it was awaiting restoration as part of the heritage fleet. The single track in Blundell Street gives access to the north end of the tram repair shop.

With Blackpool's 518-foot tower prominent in the background, Balloon car No. 706 (243) *Princess Alice* is seen passing 'OPO' car No. 7 (619/282) at Manchester Square on 2 June 1985. No. 706 is passing the old tram stop while the new LRV stop was constructed 200 metres further north, on the other side of the junction with Lytham Road. The Balloon had just re-entered service following a rebuild to open-top format after its accident in 1980. Meanwhile No. 7 was used as a basis to form replica Vanguard open bench car No. 619 just two years later (see p. 34).

Seen on 13 October 1990, Brush Railcoach No. 631 (294) is showing Manchester Square as it peels off across the Promenade road on its way to the depot. No. 631 continued in service until the final year and passed to the heritage fleet in 2012. Renovated and repainted in the 1958 livery in 2013 it has been a regular performer for the heritage fleet ever since.

Above and below: Tram Tours have been a feature of the tramway for many years with the Fylde Tramway Society (FTS) running such tours on an annual basis. These two pictures feature Coronation car No. 660 (324), in appalling weather conditions, on 2 January 1982. No. 660 was one of a batch of twenty-five trams which were built by Charles Roberts of Wakefield in 1953. They were not particularly successful and had short working lives with the tramway. The majority were withdrawn between 1968 and 1971 and broken up at various tramway premises, including Thornton Gate. In the picture above No. 660 is about to cross the Promenade at Foxhall into Princess Street, while below it is seen gingerly turning from Princess Street into Blundell Street. The crossover at Foxhall was taken out of use as part of the tramway upgrade works and although the track largely remains in Princess Street/Blundell Street the overhead current wires have been removed. Three Coronation cars, Nos 641/60/3 were still extant in 2020 and were among the pool of stored trams.

Above and below: A summer day in Blackpool in August 1995 and while the Promenade may not be teeming with day trippers the trams are out in force. In the above picture Balloon car No. 704 (241) is following No. 726 (263) towards Central Pier while below can be seen replica Vanguard car No. 619 about to pass 'OPO' car No. 762 (latterly Balloon car No. 714), which is on its way to the Pleasure Beach. No. 619 was originally English Electric Railcoach No. 282; it was withdrawn from service in April 1972 and extensively modified as 'OPO' car No. 7 (see p. 32), re-entering service as such in July 1973. No. 7 was withdrawn in 1987 and was then transferred to the Mode Wheel Workshops at Salford where it was rebuilt in its current form. It returned to Blackpool, where it operated until 2004 and then again in 2008 for the period of the Illuminations. It has been resident at Heaton Park since June 2010. Central Pier was opened on 30 May 1868 and is 371 yards long. The Ferris wheel is 108 feet in diameter and was erected in 1990, following strengthening work to the central section of the pier.

Progress Twin-Car No. 672+682 is seen at Central Pier on 27 September 2010 on its way to Little Bispham where it will use the loop to turn round. No. 672 was originally EE Railcoach No. 272 while the trailer was one of ten which were built by Metro-Cammell in 1960 and were originally numbered T1–10. This set was working in Metro Coastlines livery.

Also seen at Central Pier, but after the upgrade of the tramway and exactly five years later, is Open Boat car No. 602 (227), now part of the heritage fleet. Having first been painted black and yellow (the mini-bus livery) in 1989 it continued in service until 2010. Following refurbishment in 2013 it was painted as above, reflecting the previous tram colours which pre-dated the introduction of the Boat cars in 1934. The Tower takes centre stage as usual.

Brush Railcoach No. 637 (300) is seen marooned on the Promenade, opposite Central Pier, on 21 October 1984, having derailed due to an accumulation of sand on the track. After the incident it was used as a driver training tram but eventually returned to service in 1986 and continued to ride the tracks until it was finally withdrawn in November 2004. No. 637 departed Rigby Road in February 2012 and is now privately owned.

During the 1990s the five operational Boat cars were all painted in different colour schemes. Number 604 (230) was painted in a rendition of the red and white 'Routemaster' livery. It is seen near the Tower on 16 June 1990 heading for Talbot Square; the Open Boats were generally used between the Pleasure Beach and Cabin. Also in the picture is Balloon car No. 718 (255) and Centenary car No. 644. Number 604 was repainted into standard fleet livery in 1998 and is now part of the heritage fleet.

Above and below: By coincidence, rather than by design, Balloon car No. 717 (254) features a number of times in this account as the book traces the route of the tramway from south to north. In the picture above No. 717 is about to pass under the footbridge which used to cross the Promenade near the Tower and which can be seen in the picture below of No. 723 (260). The backdrop in the upper picture, which was recorded on 6 May 1991, shows a section of what is known as the 'Golden Mile', which started out as a succession of novelty and amusement establishments which first emerged in the late nineteenth century. No. 723 was photographed on 9 August 1995, by which time the livery application had again been revised and dayglow yellow blinds had been introduced. The footbridge, which had proved to be an admirable vantage point to view the centenary parade in 1985, was demolished in July 2009. Both of these trams formed an integral part of the operational heritage fleet in 2020.

Above and below: During the mid-1970s Blackpool Borough Transport operated a combined fleet of around 230 trams and buses. While the former tended to be the 1930s streamlined cars, supplemented by the 'OPO' Railcoach conversions, the latter still included a substantial number of 'back-loaders'. On 7 October 1978 Brush Railcoach No. 626 (289) was rubbing shoulders with an AEC Swift and MCCW-bodied Leyland PD3A/1 No. 524, opposite the Tower. Blackpool received its first Atlanteans in 1977, eventually amassing sixty-four of the type. At virtually the same location, but on 29 September 1984, Balloon car No. 726 (263), with new Centenary car No. 641 following behind, is seen heading for the Pleasure Beach, while East Lancashire-bodied Atlantean No. 357 is working on route 6 to Mereside. Number 626 left Blackpool in August 2010, bound for Merseyside, while Balloon No. 726 also left in November 2011 but returned to Rigby Road in June 2017 and was still in store in 2020.

In 1982 Brush Railcoach No. 633 (296) underwent a transformation into a mobile post office in which guise it is seen, opposite the Tower, on 29 September 1984. Stamps and postcards could be purchased on board and letters could be posted which would be franked with a special postmark. It ran in this form between 1981 and 1985 while fourteen years later it was used as the basis for the 'Trawler' feature tram.

The tramway was altered near the Tower in the 1930s to include a passing loop. This was removed, along with a similar arrangement at Talbot Square, in 2010/1 when both were replaced by a new loop situated between these two locations. On 2 September 1989 Balloon cars Nos 717 (254) and 715 (252) were photographed from the footbridge with the elegant North Pier in the background. The Cumbrian hills can also just be seen in the far distance. At least all the trams on view have a uniform appearance.

From the mid-1970s onwards Blackpool's trams were adorned with many all-over advert promotions, some of which were downright outlandish, such as this concoction which was applied to Balloon car No. 719 (256) in 1997. At the expense of the loss of a number of seats the tram was fitted with an ice-cream counter for the first two years it ran in this guise. It was photographed near the Tower on 17 August 1997. Also see picture on p. 55.

29 September 1985 was the date of the centenary parade and the crowds turned out in their thousands. One of a series of pictures recorded by the author from the vantage point of the now demolished footbridge features modified EE Railcoach Bo. 679, Jubilee car No. 762, Boat car No. 606, Glasgow Corporation Tramways No. 1297 and Sheffield Corporation Tramways No. 513. Balloon car No. 703 (240) is watching on.

The parade of trams on centenary day was made up of twenty individual trams but the star of the show was undoubtedly the John Bull steam tram which brought up the rear of the procession. The first tram in the parade was Conduit car No. 4 and by design both the first and last cars had been built in 1885. The steam tram was built by Beyer Peacock of Gorton in Manchester for the New South Wales Government Tramway. It returned to the UK in 1890 and resided at Gorton works for the next seventy years. It is now at NTM at Crich.

In 2020 both LRV Flexity trams Nos 003 and 016 carried this pink advert scheme. In the foreground is one of Blackpool's more recent attractions – the Comedy Carpet. It was officially opened by the late lamented comedian Ken Dodd on 10 October 2011. The backdrop to this picture, which was recorded on 15 March 2020, is the world famous Blackpool Tower and Ballroom, which was designed by Lancashire architects James Maxwell and Charles Tuke and opened on 14 May 1894. It is a Grade I listed building.

In the heyday of the tramway the busiest section of the line was undoubtedly between the Tower and Talbot Square. That would certainly have been true in 1976 when Balloon cars Nos 721 (258) and 709 (246) were recorded on 3 September. The iconic Lewis's store in the background, on the corner of Victoria Street, was built on the site of the Palace Theatre and was opened in 1964. However it was closed in 1993 and subsequently modified and adapted for other retail uses. No. 709 still has the twin blind apertures.

One block further along, opposite Church Street, and Balloon car No. 704 (241) is seen preceding Twin-Car No. 676+686 (276+T6), on 8 August 1997. After leaving the tramway in September 2012, No. 704 returned to Rigby Road in June 2014 and at the time of writing was actively being restored as No. 241. Similarly the 'Twin' set has remained at Blackpool, having last operated in October 2004, and was also in store at the depot in 2020.

Right and below: Not yet a third of the way along the tramway, the North Pier/ Talbot Square stop is reached after three miles. 'OPO' car No. 1 (616/269) is seen from an unusual vantage point on 2 June 1985, as the photographer has used the pier to obtain an alternative viewpoint for the picture. Only Nos 1, 5, 8 and 11 carried the later cream and green livery. No. 1 was withdrawn in 1989. In the picture below, Balloon cars Nos 722 (259) and 703 (240) can be seen at North Pier on 20 August 1995. No. 703 had recently been repainted in the wartime, mainly green, livery to celebrate fifty years since VE Day and had also had a trolley pole refitted. It was taken out of use in June 2009 and then spent seven years at the Beamish Living Museum, returning to Blackpool in March 2017 (see picture on p. 31).

A passing loop line was also provided at North Pier in the 1930s thereby providing a refuge for trams turning back towards the Pleasure Beach. A busy scene was recorded at the Pier on 26 August 1985 with Boat car No. 606 (235) having terminated while sister car No. 605 (233) is heading for Bispham; preserved Blackpool Balcony Standard car No. 40 (also see p. 85) is resting on the more recently constructed siding.

This busy scene at North Pier was recorded on the last day that trams worked through to Fleetwood, Sunday 8 November 2009, before the line closed for the upgrade works. Not a green and cream tram to be seen with Brush Railcoach No. 622 (285) taking centre stage and Balloon car No. 713 (250) and Centenary car No. 645 posed in the background. The tramway was reduced to operating between Pleasure Beach and Cleveleys from the following day. Number 622 didn't see any further service and left Blackpool for pastures new in September 2010. (Jeff Watson)

Above and below: At one time Talbot Square would have been a very busy location as trams also started from here bound for Layton (closed 1936) and Waterloo Road (Royal Oak) via Marton (closed 1962). The centre line in the Promenade route was long enough to accommodate a number of trams but on 27 June 1981 Brush Railcoach No. 630 (293) was the sole occupant. The following year, on 14 August, 'OPO' car No. 10 (614/267) was photographed on the Starr Gate to Fleetwood service. No. 10 had been English Electric Railcoach No. 614 which was modified in 1975; it was withdrawn in 1993. Partially hidden in both views is the cenotaph that was erected in 1923, while also visible in the lower view is one of the extraordinarily long passenger waiting shelters that used to exist at this stop. The new arrangement at this location now features staggered platforms with the southbound stop being to the south of the pier.

Adorned with a 'Pretty Little Thing' advert, LRV Flexity 2 No. 016 was photographed on 25 August 2019 while waiting to depart the North Pier/Talbot Road tram stop. As can clearly be seen, there was insufficient space to construct a platform for southbound trams on the opposite side. Blackpool's North Pier was the first of the three piers to be opened, on 21 May 1863. It is also the longest, measuring 550 yards, and is a Grade II listed building.

As this book was being compiled, the 550-metre-long tramway extension from Talbot Square to the North railway station had only partially been built. Construction work began in October 2017 and the laying of the rails and the associated highway ancillary works as far as Dickson Road had largely been completed by March 2019. However completion of the project was delayed due to problems in acquiring the land on which the terminal and other buildings were to be constructed. Demolition of the incumbent building, which had latterly been a Wilkos store, finally commenced in the autumn of 2020. Blackpool Transport Trident No. 310 was following the tracks on 31 May 2019.

Above and below: The 'Grand' Metropole Hotel (originally known as Bailey's Hotel) is the only building which sits between the tramway and the sea until the outskirts of Cleveleys is reached. Opened in 1785 it predates the tramway, which originally stopped some 190 yards to the north of the hotel, by 100 years. Consequently for many years the trams had to vie with motor vehicles as they rounded the obstruction. Originally a single line, there was a passing loop alongside the hotel and one at the end of the line at the junction of Cocker Street. On 16 August 1981 Balloon car No. 718 (255) follows the tracks into the main carriageway. A solution to keep the tramway separate from the road was finally implemented when the tramway was upgraded in 2012; LRV Flexity 2 No. 011 is seen at the same location on 25 August 2019. Having been modified in 2002, No. 718 is now part of the heritage fleet.

Above and below: Two views of trams drifting by the Metropole, taken some thirty-seven years apart. Still looking quite pristine and devoid of adverts, Jubilee car No. 761 was photographed heading for the Pleasure Beach on 14 August 1982. Originally Balloon car No. 725, the first of the two rebuilt cars entered service in July 1979. It differed from No. 762 markedly in only having entrances at the ends of the tram. Having had four different names during its 240 or so years of existence, the Metropole was extensively refurbished in 2018. Heritage Balloon car No. 723 (260) was a mere eighty-four years old when it was photographed on 25 August 2019. When built, the Balloons had seating for eighty-four passengers. This was later increased to ninety-four with the provision of end bench seats in the upper saloons.

Progress Twin-Car No. 677+687 (277+T7) is pursued by Boat car No. 604 (230) as it leaves the reserved track section to round the Metropole Hotel on 18 July 1989. Just opposite No. 604 is Cocker Street where the original 1885-built tramway ended. It was extended through to join the B&FTC at the Gynn in May 1900.

Holidaymakers board 'OPO' tram No. 4 at the Cocker Street tram stop on 29 September 1984, no doubt heading for the Pleasure Beach. Built in October 1972, No. 4 had originally been EE Railcoach No. 220 (608). Most of the early 'OPO' cars were soon replaced by the Centenary trams and No. 4 was withdrawn and scrapped in 1987.

The section of tramway along the North Shore to the Gynn had originally been laid in the roadway. However it was re-laid on a paved reservation in 1924. Balloon car No. 701 (238) was photographed heading south on 29 September 1984. No. 701 is now part of the active heritage fleet and is painted red and white.

This busy scene was recorded opposite Wilton Parade tram stop on the North Shore on 16 August 1981. Progress Twin-Car No. 676+686 (276+T6) leads Balloon No. 700 (237), both no doubt carrying excited passengers bound for the Pleasure Beach. All four trams in this scene are painted in the 1970s livery. The Illumination's tableaux are ready in place for the big switch on in three weeks time. To the right is the newly built Pembroke hotel (known as the Grand in 2020), which didn't open until the following year.

Above and below: These two scenes were recorded at the same location and both during the period of the illuminations, although twenty-eight years apart. LRV Flexity 2 No. 014, in all-over advert livery for JD Sports, is seen on 25 October 2018, while Open Boat car No. 607 (236) is heading for the Cabin on 16 September 1990. No. 607 was withdrawn from service in July 2004 and left Blackpool in 2012 for the National Tramway Museum at Crich in Derbyshire where it is now part of the museum collection. The Grand Hotel name is prominent in the upper picture while the old Pembroke name can be seen in the lower picture. In-between the hotel was also known as the Stakis (1996–99) and the Hilton (1999–2018). Prominent in both views is Blackpool Tower, which stands at 518 feet 9 inches (158.1 metres) tall and can actually be seen from as far away as Pendle Hill (30 miles) and the Forest of Bowland (27 miles) on a clear day.

Above and below: Two mid-1980s views on the North Promenade, close to Gynn Square. Brush Railcoach No. 632 (295) was new in August 1937. As depicted on the tram in this September 1984 view, Wilson's Brewery commenced brewing beer in 1834 from premises in Newton Heath, Manchester. The brewery was amalgamated with Watney Mann in 1960 but ceased brewing in 1987. Meanwhile No. 632 was withdrawn in November 2011 and after a short period of storage at Marton it returned to Rigby Road in December 2013 where it currently resides. Below, Open Boat car No. 605 is seen on a gloriously sunny 2 June 1985. This tram was subsequently preserved and after a spell at the Beamish Museum it was shipped across the Atlantic and is now operated by Muni in San Francisco.

Depicting the modern scene at the same location is LRV Flexity 2 No. 013, recorded on 22 June 2019. This view clearly shows how the tracks have been renewed and laid on a newly formed permanent way.

When the tramway was modernised the Gynn tram stop was relocated approximately 100 metres to the north so that the platforms could be constructed on a straight section of track. Centenary car No. 643 was photographed at the old southbound tram stop on 16 June 1990. Withdrawn in 2011, No. 643 first saw use as a cafe at a nearby caravan park before moving on to the West Midlands. By 2020 the Maxime Hotel had changed to the Rose Hotel & Spa but the last five digits of the telephone number remained the same.

Above and below: In 1938 the layout at Gynn Square was much different than it was in 2020, or indeed in 1984 when the above picture was recorded. There was no roundabout and in addition to the double track there was a passing loop line on the southbound side. The double track line leading into Dickson Road (the original B&FTC line) diverged just to the north of this loop. 'OPO' car No. 2 (620/283) is followed by Balloon No. 715 (252) on 29 September 1984. While No. 2 was scrapped in January 1987, the Balloon is now part of the heritage fleet. Although the stops had been moved, the layout remained the same when LRV Flexity 2 No. 010 was photographed passing heritage Balloon car No. 713, on 22 June 2019. Designed by Thomas Gallon Lumb (1862–1953), the Savoy Hotel was opened in 1915 and is a Grade II listed building.

A southbound view at the Gynn shows the S-bend to good effect as it sweeps down grade. Balloon No. 719 (256) is seen approaching the old tram stop on a grey Saturday 26 September 1992. It was modified with widened doors in 1996 when it also lost its curved front and end side windows (also see picture on p. 40) and is now one of the three Balloons in the heritage fleet that were painted purple and white in 2012.

Heading north the tramway climbs from Gynn Square towards the Cabin. Progress Twin-Car No. 675+685 (275+T5) is one of two of the type which has seen service with the heritage fleet. It is seen on a 'limited stop tour' bound for Fleetwood on 27 September 2015. This car has been finished in the 1960s half green/half cream livery.

Above and below: Two views recorded at the Cliffs Hotel on 17 October 1992. Balloon car No. 700 (237), painted in the livery of the era, has just departed the tram stop with a full load of holidaymakers heading for the Promenade and Pleasure Beach. Behind, Centenary car No. 646 is mopping up the large queue but as can be seen in the view below there are still three passengers left at the stop. However Twin-Car No. 675+685 is thankfully not far behind. The Centenary trams were taken out of service in 2011 when the tramway closed for upgrade work to be carried out. No. 646 was initially sold but suffered from vandalism and was subsequently scrapped. At this point the tramway is a significant height above the lower walkway and a lift is provided at the Cabin (see p. 57) to access the lower level.

The long-standing crossover at the Cabin was retained but is now principally used by the heritage trams, some of which turn back here. Balloon car No 712 (249) is seen painted in a different livery application from the picture on p. 17. Recorded on 8 September 1991, Centenary car No. 647 is the tram in hot pursuit.

LRV Flexity 2 No. 018 had only been in service for a matter of days when it was photographed at the Cabin on 5 April 2018. The lift to the lower walk can be seen on the left. Built in 1930, it is now a Grade II listed building and originally took passengers down to an enclosed boating pool that was situated between the sea wall and the lower walk.

This scene was recorded at the Cabin on 21 October 1984 and features preserved Coronation Car No. 660 (324) and then relatively new Centenary car No. 641; the occasion was a Fylde Tramway Society (FTS) tour. No. 660 is one of three survivors of the class and was in store at Rigby Road depot in 2020.

Another view at the Cabin recorded at the height of the illuminations on 14 October 1990. Twin-Car No. 671+681 (271+T1) has most likely turned on the loop at Little Bispham while Balloon car No. 713 (250) is waiting on the centre road to follow it south. No. 713 was the first of the second batch of Balloons and entered service in December 1934. Meanwhile the Twin-Car has been in store at Rigby Road since 2016.

The Cabin is again the setting for this scene recorded on 18 July 1989. Brush Railcoach No. 634 (297) is about to depart for Fleetwood while Boat car No. 606 (235) sits on the centre road and is about to have its trolley pole reversed for the run back to the Tower or the Pleasure Beach. No. 606 was painted in this blue and yellow livery the previous year before making a guest appearance at the Glasgow Garden Festival. It was withdrawn in 2000 and exported to the United States with Standard No. 147 making the reverse trip.

The second of the additional pair of LRV Flexity 2 trams, No. 017, is seen approaching the Cabin on 28 May 2018. The separate stop for the heritage trams can be seen between the first two sections of the tram. Following the tramway upgrade and the previous work carried out in 2008 to remove the centre turn back road the layout at this location was extensively simplified.

The track between the Cabin and Bispham is laid on sleepers and is completely segregated from both road traffic and pedestrians. Consequently trams can attain a reasonable speed on this section. Heritage Centenary car No. 648 is doing just that as it heads for Little Bispham on 27 May 2018. The shelter is one of a series of four which date from around 1905 and are listed buildings.

LRV Flexity 2 No. 003 is seen opposite the Miners Home on 15 March 2020, just eight days before the country went into lockdown for ten weeks due to the COVID-19 pandemic. The tram has just passed through the Lowther Avenue stop while in the distance can be seen the Cabin Lift. The stops at St Stephen's Avenue and the Miners Home, on this stretch, were abolished when the tramway was upgraded.

Brush Railcoach No. 631 (294) is seen heading south past the former Miners Home (which is on the opposite side of the road) on 27 May 2018. It has been an active member of the heritage fleet since 2013.

A chance meeting of heritage cars was captured at Bispham on 15 March 2020. Railcoach No. 621 (284) left Blackpool in December 2011 and was initially stored at Kirkham Prison prior to moving to Beamish before arriving back at Rigby Road five years later. Following restoration it re-entered service in September 2017. Balloon car No. 717 (254) was retired from service at the end of the 2003 season but was subsequently refurbished to near 1930s condition in 2008 and was retained by the heritage fleet after retirement from normal service.

Above and below: On May Bank Holiday Monday in 1981 this impressive line of trams was photographed at rest on the centre road at Bispham. Comprising Railcoaches Nos 627, 680, 626, 621 and Balloons Nos 718 and 722, it will be noted that all six trams still have their trolley poles and that the poles are all facing the same way. Also seen in the centre road, but twenty years later, Railcoaches Nos 678 (278) and 632 (295), fitted with pantographs, were photographed on 11 August 2000. The former was one of the second series of cars built by English Electric in 1935. It was withdrawn in 1961 and following modification work it ran with trailer T8 as a Twin-Car until 1972 when the trailer was scrapped. No. 678 is now owned by the Fleetwood Heritage Leisure Trust and is in store awaiting restoration.

Balloon Car No. 707 (244) was the first of four of the type to be rebuilt in this form and rechristened as Millennium Cars. It is seen at Bispham on 11 August 2000. Across the road can be seen the Royal Bank of Scotland on the corner of Red Bank Road. A single track used to diverge just in front of where the tram is standing, which led to Bispham tram depot some 300 yards along the road. Opened by the B&FTC in 1898 the six road depot was closed in 1966. The site is now occupied by a supermarket store.

The importance of the stabling road at Bispham is demonstrated again as 'OPO' Car No. 8 (612/265) was photographed passing No. 762 (714/251) on 16 June 1984. No. 8 entered service in its rebuilt form in June 1974 and continued in service until 1992. It is one of two of the type that were still extant in 2020. No. 762 is now preserved at the National Tramway Museum in Crich. The centre road was retained following the tramway upgrade.

Heritage Standard car No. 147 was photographed at Bispham on 28 May 2018. The picture also depicts the art deco shelter which was built in 1932 and was intended as a rest centre for tram crews between duties. It was equipped with a toilet, brewing up facilities and accommodation for a Duty Inspector. Cafe facilities had been incorporated into the building by 2020.

The reserved track continues north between Bispham and Little Bispham. Balloon car No. 709 (246) is seen approaching Norbreck North on 25 May 1981. Four of the original five stops (Norbreck was upgraded) on this section were closed in 2011 but a new stop was opened in 2012 and a previously closed stop was reopened in 2016, with all three having raised platforms for LRV use. No. 709 was rebuilt as a Millennium tram in 2000.

Above and below: 'OPO' Car No. 8 (612/265) is seen again at Little Bispham on 14 July 1991. Now painted green and cream it was in its penultimate year of service with the municipal undertaking. The excessive overhang combined with the additional weight resulted in the cabs drooping with age as can be seen in this broadside view. Consequently the type had a fairly low age profile. The 1935-built art deco brick tram shelter survived the upgrade works and now incorporates toilet facilities. Seen on the same day is Balloon car No. 700 (237) with a near full load heading for Fleetwood. The tram was modified with widened doorways in 2010 and is now in the purple and white colour scheme as part of the 'B' fleet. Note that in this view No. 700 is still equipped with a trolley pole and has the original roof light windows, the latter a feature which the tram has retained.

A number of events were staged during the centenary year. The turning circle at Little Bispham was constructed in 1937 and is the setting for this gathering of trams on 5 May 1985. Preserved 1902-built Dreadnought tram No. 59 (also see p. 94) was resident on the tramway between 1960 and 1965 and 1975 and 1990. Behind is Balcony Standard car No. 40, which operated on the tramway from 1926 to 1963. Both these trams are now part of the national collection. Completing the line-up are Balloon car No. 706 (243) and Coronation No. 660 (324).

In the first of three views featuring Open Boat car No. 606 (235) on an FTS tour on 11 May 1980, the tram is seen at Little Bispham on the rarely used short section of track which leads from the turning circle to the main line in a northerly direction. No. 606 was exported to the United States in September 2000. It is now resident at the National Capital Trolley Museum in Maryland.

Above and below: In the past the turning circle was particularly useful for turning the Twin-Cars. Retained on the transit system it is now almost exclusively used by the heritage trams. These two views were recorded at almost the exact same location. Above, LRV Flexity 2 No. 015 is seen heading south to Starr Gate on 24 February 2018. Some thirty-seven years earlier, on 25 May 1981, Balloon car No. 710 (247) was on a similar duty but only going as far as the Pleasure Beach. The Pitch & Putt golf course (seen behind No. 710) has since disappeared, as has the green hoarding (in 2020), to reveal a children's play area. The arrangement of the catenary support poles is slightly different with a number having been repositioned outside the concrete fence. No. 710 was withdrawn in 2007 and left the tramway in 2010. It is now part of the Fleetwood Heritage Leisure Trust collection. It was also the tram which featured in a dramatic episode of *Coronation Street* in 1989.

The two trams featured on the tour on p. 58 are seen again on their way back from Fleetwood. Centenary car No. 641 is now leading Coronation tram No. 660 at Little Bispham. No. 641 is advertising the forthcoming centenary celebrations and its East Lancashire Coachbuilder's lineage.

On arrival at Cleveleys the tram would have travelled almost exactly 7 miles along the coast from Starr Gate. Two of the first batch of Balloon cars, Nos 705 (242) and 708 (245) have arrived at their destination on 3 July 1976 and will be turning back towards Blackpool. No. 705 was the third of the type to be withdrawn (after Nos 714/25 which were rebuilt as the Jubilee trams) following a collision with No. 706 at the Pleasure Beach in July 1980. No. 708 was in store at Rigby Road at the time of writing.

The Metro Coastlines branding with different liveries for separate routes was introduced in 2001 and was mainly intended for the buses. However a number of trams were also painted accordingly. Balloon car No. 713 (250), seen waiting at Cleveleys to depart for Starr Gate on 9 May 2008, was one of four of the type to receive different Metro liveries.

LRV Flexity 2 No. 004 waits at the northbound platform at Cleveleys on 27 September 2015 with a journey bound for Fleetwood. Adjacent, Blackpool Transport Trident No. 329 can be seen working on the parallel bus service which also runs from Starr Gate to Fleetwood.

LRV Flexity 2 No. 007 was photographed crossing the busy Victoria Road in the centre of Cleveleys as it leaves the tram stop behind on 8 July 2014. When the tramway was first opened in 1898 the expanse of land behind the tram was nothing more than open fields and the parallel roadway on the left did not exist.

Two well-loaded trams are seen waiting to leave Cleveleys on 23 April 1984. Brush Railcoach No. 621 (284) is only going as far as Talbot Square; it is now part of the heritage fleet. Behind and bound for Starr Gate is 'OPO' car No. 12 (611/264). The penultimate conversion, No. 12 entered service in June 1975. It was withdrawn in 1988 and subsequently scrapped.

The track layout at Cleveleys was fairly straight forward with just the up and down roads and a simple crossover for trams terminating there. A significant number of journeys used to turn back at Cleveleys. Balloon car No. 717 (254) has just used the facility for its return journey to the Pleasure Beach on 25 May 1981. It will be noted that separate shelters were provided for waiting and disembarking passengers. No. 717 is now part of the active heritage fleet.

Following the upgrade of the tramway the shelters and crossover were removed and two standard raised platforms were constructed. No trams now terminate at Cleveleys although it is an alighting/boarding point for both LRVs and heritage trams. LRV Flexity 2 No. 001 is seen heading for Starr Gate on 25 August 2018.

Above and below: After leaving Cleveleys the tramway runs parallel with Rossall Road/ Broadway (A587) as far as Rossall Lane where it then diverges across open land. While the tram stop at Beach Road was closed, West Drive (before Thornton Gate is reached) was upgraded. In the picture above, recorded on 14 August 1982, Railcoach No. 636 (299) is seen passing Balloon car No. 715 (252) at the exact position where the new Thornton Gate platforms have since been constructed. In the lower view, recorded on 24 September 2017, LRV Flexity 2 No. 010 and heritage Balloon car No. 723 are seen in the same place but viewed from the opposite direction. Cumberland Avenue crosses in the foreground. No. 636 was sold to a company in Derby to be used as a test tram and left Blackpool in 2006 while No. 715 is now part of the heritage fleet.

Heritage Balloon car No. 701 is seen waiting to cross Cumberland Avenue at Thornton Gate on 15 July 2018. Again, when the tramway was constructed there was nothing but open fields to the right and Cumberland Avenue did not exist.

The sidings at Thornton Gate were constructed by Blackpool Corporation five years after the Corporation took over the Blackpool & Fleetwood Tramroad Company, in January 1920. The site was used as a Permanent Way (PW) depot where rails and other tramway equipment were stored; a number of trams including Coronations, Standards and Railcoaches were also broken up at this location. Open Boat car No. 606 (235) is again seen on the FTS tour on 11 May 1980, within the confines of the PW depot.

This somewhat unusual photograph depicts seven of the thirteen 'OPO' cars at Thornton Gate on an unrecorded date and is thought to date from 1987. The two trams nearest the camera are Nos 2 (620/283) and 9 (613/266). The layout of the track with the centre road and crossover can be clearly seen and compared with the layout in the lower picture after the upgrade works were carried out. (Fylde Tramway Society)

The track layout in 2018 didn't look that much different. The area between the rails has been finished in reinforced concrete. The PW depot has been closed and the land fenced off. Heritage trams, which terminate at Cleveleys, now use the centre road here to turn back. LRV Flexity 2 No. 002 was recorded heading south on 27 May 2018.

The restoration of Bolton car No. 66 was a prolonged affair and the tram is privately owned, first coming to the Blackpool Tramway in 1981. With agreement between the owners and Blackpool Transport Services it has remained there ever since. On 27 May 2018 it was photographed alongside Kendal Avenue at Thornton Gate/Rossall. The Westmorland Avenue stop at this location was closed in 2010.

Kendal Avenue leads into Milnthorpe Avenue (on the right), which is where Balloon car No. 709 (246) (see also pages 42 and 64) was photographed on 14 August 1982. The stop here, known as Rossall Beach, was upgraded to LRT standard as part of the upgrade works.

Balloon Car No. 711 (248) has just passed the Westbourne Road stop on its journey south from Fleetwood on 31 July 1981. This scene presents a very rural picture with cows grazing in the adjacent field. In 2020 the landscape was much the same but the tram stop no longer existed. See p. 11 for a picture of No. 711 in its present guise.

Proceeding north after Westbourne Road the next stop was Rossall School followed by Rossall Square, which is where Balloon car No. 715 (252) was photographed on 15 August 1982. while the narrow southbound LRT platform was constructed adjacent to where the tram can be seen; the northbound platform is equally narrow but is on the opposite side of South Strand. Not much room to spare – it could not have been envisaged when the houses were built that platforms would later be built at this stop.

Above and below: Broadwater is the next stop heading north and is situated where the tramway crosses Fleetwood Road at an acute angle. It was named after the nearby Broadwater Wood and had previously been known simply as the Fleetwood Road station with a waiting shelter located alongside the tram stop shown in the upper picture. Three of the ten rebuilt English Electric Railcoaches lost their trailers as far back as 1972 and continued in service as single unit trams. No. 678 (278) was photographed at Broadwater on 14 August 1982 while similar tram No. 680 (280) was recorded on 28 May 2018, by which time it was operating on loan from the Heaton Park Tramway as part of the heritage fleet. It had last seen regular service in Blackpool in 2009.

Above and below: LRV Flexity 2 No. 003 was photographed at Broadwater on 15 March 2017. In the far distance the manufacturing plant of the world famous Fisherman's Friend lozenges can just be glimpsed. The view of LRV Flexity 2 No. 017 below is looking in the opposite direction and was recorded on 28 May 2018. Again the tram stop was relocated and the LRT platforms can just be seen beyond the tram. This is quite a complicated junction with two other roads also converging and consequently road traffic is regulated by conventional traffic signals.

This chance shot of heritage tram Standard No. 147 and LRV Flexity 2 No. 002, about to cross at Broadwater, was again recorded on 28 May 2018. The drivers of the modern day LRVs are afforded the luxury of a seated position in front of their consoles (see inset) while the drivers of the first generation trams have to stand at their controllers.

Captured on the same day as Railcoach No. 678, 14 August 1982, was Balloon car No. 707 (244) (see p. 63 for a view of this tram in its rebuilt form). Broadwater post office was still open for business in 2020 but the K6 telephone kiosk had been removed without replacement. No. 707 has been retained as part of the 'B' fleet.

Of the four stops between Broadwater and Ash Street only one was closed with the other three being upgraded with raised platforms. Ash Street itself has been renamed Fisherman's Walk. Another tram which paid a visit to Blackpool in centenary year was Sheffield Corporation Tramways 1952 stylish Roberts-built car No. 513. It is seen at the Ash Street stop on tram Sunday which was held on 14 July that year.

By 2018 the annual Fleetwood extravaganza had been renamed the Fleetwood Festival of Transport. As in previous years the section of line through the town centre to the ferry was closed and LRV Flexity 2 No. 001 is seen crossing over to the southbound track on 15 July for its return journey to Starr Gate. Balloon car No. 700 can be seen in the background in use as a control vehicle and mobile shop.

Ash Street again on 14 July 1985. Balloon car No. 711 (248) has arrived from Blackpool while preserved Pantograph car No. 167 is working a shuttle service to Fleetwood Ferry. The Pantographs were introduced in 1928 and were originally known as Pullman cars. No. 167 was withdrawn from service in July 1953 and then served as a PW car until 1962, when it was donated to the National Tramway Museum for restoration.

There is no mistaking where this picture was taken. This is tram Sunday again, but in July 2002, and rebuilt English Electric Railcoach No. 680 (280) (see also p. 77) is waiting to depart for Starr Gate. No. 680 is one of six former Blackpool Trams now owned by the Heaton Park Tramway, the others being Nos 619/23, 702/8 and rail grinder No. 1(752). The B&FTC Copse Road six road tram depot was situated just 500 yards or so in the distance on the left. It was closed in 1963 and after being used as a venue for other businesses the building was eventually demolished in 2016.

Above and below: Two studies in black and white captured by the photographer in Lord Street (formerly West Street and East Street) on Saturday 27 June 1981. Both views portray a busy and bustling town centre atmosphere. In the above picture 'OPO' car No. 4 (608/220) is seen passing the junction of Styan Street and is making the full line journey to Starr Gate. At this time the core service was firmly in the hands of the 'OPO' cars and another of the type, No. 8 (612/265), is seen approaching the photographer's view point of the inside of a Brush Railcoach, which is travelling in the opposite direction. On the right is St Mary's RC Church. The tram stops at Preston Street and Church Street were both closed in 2009 and replaced by one at London Street, which crosses Lord Street behind the Railcoach, for use by the LRVs. In 2020 Fleetwood was a somewhat quieter place.

The National Westminster Bank again identifies this location as the junction of Styan Street. Brush Railcoach No. 631 (294) (also see pages 32 and 61) was photographed heading south on 2 July 1983. No. 631 was in its forty-sixth year of service having been introduced in August 1937. It would carry on giving another twenty-eight years service for BBT/BTS.

LRV Flexity 2 No. 011 is seen passing the site of the former Preston Street tram stop in Lord Street on 20 August 2015. In conjunction with the upgrade of the tramway the whole of Lord Street benefitted from an extensive highway renovation scheme which included resurfacing of the carriageway, block paving and the provision of parking bays and raised brick planters. The LRV is just approaching the new London Street tram stop.

In the early years of the Fleetwood Festival (Tram Sunday) a shuttle service was provided between Fleetwood Ferry and Ash Street using vintage trams. Pantograph car No. 167 and Sheffield CT No. 513 are depicted in Lord Street on 14 July 1985. Preserved buses from the erstwhile fleets of Southdown and Salford City Transport are also in attendance.

Back in time again to Saturday 27 June 1981 and the last of the Balloon cars, No. 726 (263), is seen in Lord Street passing the junction of Warren Street. Balloon cars were not an unfamiliar sight in Fleetwood, particularly on market days which were held on Tuesday, Thursday, Friday and Saturday. By 2020 the Children's Corner shop was trading as Studio Nails.

Blackpool Corporation Standard No. 40 was withdrawn from service in January 1963 after giving thirty-seven years of service with the undertaking. It then moved to the NTM at Crich but paid an extended visit to its home town in 1985. Posed alongside St Peter's Church on 5 May 1985, it is about to be passed by 'OPO' car No. 3 (610/224). The latter was withdrawn and scrapped within the next couple of years.

St Peter's Church dominates Albert Square and was consecrated in 1841 and is now a Grade II listed building. It was designed by the architect Decimus Burton (1800–81), one of the foremost English architects and urban designers of the nineteenth century. LRV Flexity 2 No. 007 was caught sweeping round the curve into North Albert Street on a wet November Sunday in 2017.

Above and below: The background to these two pictures, recorded thirty-seven years apart, has hardly changed. Only the occupancy and the outside appearance of the buildings are different. The location is again Albert Square as it leads into North Albert Street. Above, it is market day again and Balloon cars Nos 724 (261) and 711 (248) were photographed passing on Friday 31 July 1981. No. 724 was rebuilt in 2004 when it was fitted with modified doors. It was the last of the four rebuilds which were reclassified as Millennium cars. In 2020 the tram was in store at Rigby Road as part of the 'B' fleet. Meanwhile in the picture below LRV Flexity 2 No. 006 is seen in splendid isolation with hardly a sole to be seen on a crisp and bright Sunday morning in February 2018.

Brush Railcoach No. 625 (288) was photographed in North Albert Street, approaching Albert Square, on 27 June 1981. It is seen against a backdrop of Victorian brick buildings and what might be considered forty years later to be an assortment of vintage cars. After leaving the Blackpool Tramway in December 2011 and although privately owned it returned to Rigby Road for storage in June 2017.

Most of the buildings in the picture above again feature in this view of LRV Flexity 2 No. 011 which is seen at the Victoria Street stop in North Albert Street on 26 November 2017. This stop and the previous stop in Lord Street were the only two bi-directional new tram stops which had to be accommodated within the confines of a built-up road layout.

For the final time we see Boat car No. 606 (235) on the FTS tour of 11 May 1980. It is pictured on the little used crossover before the junction of North Albert Street and Kent Street. A new crossover was installed on the other side of the junction when this section of the tramway was upgraded in 2010.

For this July 1985 view the photographer has crossed the road but is still looking north. Preserved Hyde Road-built 1914 Manchester Corporation Tramways No. 765 is seen near the junction with Arthur Street as it heads for the ferry terminus in Queen's Terrace. It was part of a batch of five fitted with Brill trucks with seating for forty passengers. It was withdrawn by MCT in 1930. Balloon car No. 706 *Princess Alice* can be seen in the distance passing the junction of Pharos Street where the tracks split.

Above and below: When the Blackpool and Fleetwood Tramroad opened on 14 July 1898 the line ended at the junction of Bold Street. There were two crossovers between the two tracks which actually lead into a small depot, built on land which had formerly been part of an army barracks and which had a capacity for just four trams (the building at the end of the road partially occupies the old depot site). The layout was radically altered in 1924 when a single loop line was laid along North Albert Street and Bold Street to Queen's Terrace where the trams terminated. It then returned via Pharos Street to North Albert Street. In the above picture, taken on 29 June 1985, Balloon car No. 720 (257) is just approaching the split while in the picture below, which dates from 31 July 1981, sister car No. 718 (255) is approaching what was originally the end of the line. Note how the livery application has changed in the intervening years.

In 2006 the Pleasure Beach decided to stop advertising on the trams and consequently the previous year's adverts were removed from Balloons Nos 715/21 and the trams were painted white. No. 721 (258) was photographed in Bold Street on 6 July 2006. It was withdrawn in November 2009 and was bought by the North Eastern Electrical Traction Trust and was transported to their base in Sunderland for restoration, in March 2012.

The old tram stop was for alighting only and the trams would wait time in Queen's Terrace. Centenary tram No. 647 is also pictured in Bold Street but some eleven years earlier, on 9 August 1995. By coincidence No. 647 is now also owned by the NEETT, as is Twin-Car set No. 674+684.

The new LRT tram stop was constructed where the previous alighting stop had been located but only one platform was required since this section of the tramway is single line. The impressive looking North Euston Hotel can be seen in the background. Also designed by Decimus Burton, it was commissioned by local landowner Peter Hesketh-Fleetwood and opened in August 1841 with the intention that it would be used by travellers making their onward journey to Scotland by boat as at that time there was no railway line in the north of the county. 11 miles and fifty-eight minutes after leaving Starr Gate LRV Flexity 2 No. 005 has arrived at journey's end, on 25 February 2018.

As previously recounted the loop line at Fleetwood was constructed in 1924 and two tracks were provided in Queen's Terrace so that trams could pass. Balloon No. 722 (259) was waiting to depart for Starr Gate on a somewhat overcast 31 July 1981. No. 722 was withdrawn in 2007 following an accident and is one of only three Balloon cars to have been scrapped, the others being Nos 705/16.

Brush Railcoaches Nos 622 (285) and 636 (299), in contrasting colour schemes and both still with trolley poles, wait time in Queen's Terrace on 12 July 1985. Both of these trams left Blackpool a number of years ago. Also in the picture is Ribble's dual-door Leyland National No. 381 which was allocated to Fleetwood garage at the time. The view behind the trams looks across Morecambe Bay to the Furness Peninsula.

When the tracks were renewed they were placed slightly further apart. LRV Flexity 2 No. 009 was traversing the outside track in Queen's Terrace when photographed on 15 March 2017. The buildings in the background have changed little over the years and even the small ice-cream outlet with its roof lettering was still there in 2020. The word 'FERRY' can just be seen adjacent to the roof of the tram – the Knott End Ferry which crosses the mouth of the Wyre estuary was inaugurated sometime during the 1890s and a half-hourly frequency service, between 07.45 and 17.45, was advertised in October 2020.

Glasgow Corporation Tramways No. 1297 was another visitor to Blackpool during the centenary year. No. 1297 has been resident at the Crich Tramway Museum since July 1963, having been withdrawn from service in September 1962. It was built in Glasgow's Coplawhill Works in 1948 and was one of a series of one hundred trams which were known as Cunarders. It is seen parked in the company of Balloon car No. 724 and preserved Edinburgh Corporation Tramways No. 35 (also see p. 19), on 14 July 1985.

Centenary car No. 645 was photographed turning from Queen's Terrace into Pharos Street on 24 September 1997. From 1998 onwards most of these trams were modified which included restyling of the front ends; No. 645 was so treated in 2003. It was withdrawn following the final day of service of the old tramway on 6 November 2011. In 2020 it was in store at Rigby Road depot awaiting restoration as part of the heritage fleet.

Following the overhead electrification of the Blackpool Tramway in 1898 and the subsequent expansion of the system the department invested in forty-seven new trams over the next four years, thirty-five of which were designed by the Midland Railway Carriage & Wagon Company and built by G. F. Milnes. Twenty of these, Nos 15–26 and 54–61, were known as Dreadnoughts, named after the Royal Navy battleships of the same name. Sole survivor No. 59 is seen in Pharos Street in appropriate weather on 14 July 1985 while on loan from the NTM.

Throughout the journey from Starr Gate virtually all the department's trams of the period have been illustrated at least once. Completing the Centenary cars is No. 644, which was photographed passing the Pharos Lighthouse on 18 July 1989. It is seen in original condition having only been in service for a little over two years. It is now resident at Farmer Parr's Animal World on the outskirts of Fleetwood.

Above and below: The section of tramway from Cleveleys to Fleetwood was completely closed after 8 November 2009 although trams were able to run through to Ash Street from the following May. Works to upgrade the track and infrastructure were substantially complete on the Fleetwood section by late 2011 but it wasn't until March 2012 that the first LRV made a test run over the section. The new LRT service commenced operation on 4 April 2012 and new LRV Flexity 2 No. 008 was photographed in Pharos Street just a couple of weeks later. With the extension of the heritage service to Fleetwood in 2013 a separate stop was provided in Pharos Street. Heritage trams could, if required, wait time on the loop in Queen's Terrace to allow LRVs to pass before proceeding to the heritage stop. Following a period of enforced inactivity due to the coronavirus pandemic in 2020 operations recommenced in August. Open Boat No. 602 (227), seen below, has briefly paused at the stop while on a round tour from the Pleasure Beach, on 27 September.

Left and below: Brush Railcoach No. 627 (290) (also see pages 15 and 62) is dwarfed by the 93-foot-tall Pharos Lighthouse as it glides silently past on 29 June 1985. Built in sandstone, the lighthouse was designed by Decimus Burton and completed in 1840. Named after the ancient lighthouse Pharos of Alexandria it has a range of approximately 12 nautical miles and was managed by the Port of Fleetwood Authority in 2020. Note the Ribble Leyland National bus in the background. Very little had changed by the time LRV Flexity 2 No. 004 was photographed on 2 May 2018, although the tramway has now been segregated from the roadway.